SWIMMING
FROM DIVING TO WATER POLO
by Jason Page

TAKING THE LEAP

Martin Lopez Zubero (ESP) is shown here at the start of the Olympic 200-metres backstroke race.

AQUATIC EVENTS

*T**he newly built National Aquatic Centre in London has a seating capacity of 17,500 and pools that hold a combined total of 10 million litres of water. The centre's vast, wave-like roof will be the first thing seen by visitors to the Olympic Park.***

COOL!

The first-ever modern Olympic swimming event was the 100-metres freestyle, held in 1896. There were only 10 competitors and the race was held, not in a swimming pool, but in the icy cold waters of the Bay of Zea, off the coast of Greece. Competitors simply dived off a boat and swam to the shore! The race was won by a 19-year-old Hungarian sailor named Alfred Hajos.

SUPER STATS

There were over 1,200 athletes taking part in the aquatic events at the Beijing Olympics. Together they would have filled two jumbo jets!

FOUR OF THE BEST

Swimming events were not held at the ancient Olympics, but they have been part of the modern Games ever since they began. The proper title of this sport is 'aquatics', and it's made up of four separate disciplines: swimming, diving, water polo and synchronized swimming.

AQUATIC FIRSTS

Several new events made their Olympic debut at the 2000 Games, including synchronized diving, shown here, and women's water polo.

OLYMPICS FACT FILE

The Olympic Games were first held in Olympia, in ancient Greece, around 3,000 years ago. They took place every four years until they were abolished in 393 CE.

A Frenchman called Pierre de Coubertin (1863–1937) revived the Games, and the first modern Olympics were held in Athens in 1896.

The modern Games have been held every four years since 1896, except in 1916, 1940 and 1944, due to war. A special, unofficial 10th anniversary Games took place in Athens in 1906.

The symbol of the Olympic Games is five interlocking coloured rings. Together, they represent the five different continents from which athletes come to compete.

GOLDEN GREATS

Mark Spitz (USA) is the greatest swimmer ever seen at the Olympic Games. Between 1968 and 1972, he won a total of nine golds, a silver and a bronze. His record tally of seven victories at one Olympics is unmatched in any sport to this day!

Mark Spitz (USA)

50-METRES FREESTYLE

The 50-metres freestyle covers just one length of the pool, making it both the shortest of all the swimming races and the fastest.

THE NAME'S BIONDI...

In 1988, the men's 50-metres freestyle was won by Matt Biondi (USA), the only swimmer who has managed to win as many Olympic medals as Mark Spitz! Between 1984 and 1992, Biondi swam away with eight golds, two silvers and a bronze.

Amy Van Dyken (USA)

ANIMAL OLYMPIANS

The gold medal for sprint swimming in the animal kingdom goes to the mighty sailfish. With a top speed of 110 km/h, this super-fast fish would finish the 50-metres freestyle in just 1.6 seconds!

TOUGH COMPETITION

Amy Van Dyken is the first American woman to win four gold medals in one Olympic Games. In 1996 she won gold in the 50-metres freestyle and 100-metres butterfly events. She went to Sydney four years later and won a further two golds in the relays.

DID YOU KNOW?

An Olympic 50-metres freestyle champion swims at a top speed of 8 km/h — that's about twice as fast as your normal walking pace.

An Olympic swimming pool is 1.8 metres deep — that's deep enough to go over the head of an average adult.

The 50-metres event (or 50-yards as it was then known) first appeared at the Olympic Games in 1904. It was not held again until 1988 — 84 years later.

EARN TO CRAWL

freestyle races, any stroke n be used — but swimmers ways choose the front crawl cause it's the fastest stroke. the front crawl, one arm es over the swimmer's ad while the other is pushed wn through the water. the same time, the immer kicks their legs ickly up and down — up to kicks per arm stroke.

Alexander Popov (RUS)

POPOV'S PRIDE OF PLACE

Alexander Popov (RUS) won both the 50- and 100-metres freestyle at the 1992 and the 1996 Olympics. In 2000 he won the Silver medal for the 100-metres and still holds the Olympic and World records for the 50-metres freestyle.

Even short hair creates water resistance and slows swimmers down. That's why most swimmers wear swimming caps.

Swimmers wear goggles to protect their eyes from chemicals in the water.

Swimming costumes are made of light, flexible materials, including Teflon — also used to make non-stick frying pans!

SPEEDO

Streamlined swimming

DID YOU KNOW?

♫ The 1984 women's 100-metres freestyle final was a dead heat. Both swimmers were awarded gold medals.

♫ The swimming events at the Olympics in 1900 included a 200-metres obstacle race!

♫ Women competed in swimming events at the Olympics for the first time in 1912.

SHORT-DISTANCE FREESTYLE

*T**he 100-metres and 200-metres races give swimmers
a chance to demonstrate speed over a longer distance.***

A NEW DAWN?

Dawn Fraser (AUS) won the women's
100-metres freestyle in 1956, 1960
and 1964. She was the first swimmer
ever to win an Olympic gold in the
same event three times in a row.

Dawn Fraser (AUS)

SPLIT-SECOND TIMING

Swimming races are timed electronically. The signal to start the race
automatically starts the clock. As each swimmer touches the
wall at the end of the race, a pressure pad records their
time to within one hundredth of a second!

GET OUT OF MY WAY!

In 1920, the final of the
men's 100-metres freestyle
had to be swum again after an
Australian competitor complained that
one of the US competitors had impeded
him. However, it made no difference to
the result as both races were won by
Duke Kahanamoku (USA). He broke the
world record in the first race and then
matched his time in the re-run!

SUPER STATS

The pool used
at the Olympic
Games is 50 metres long
– almost double the length of two
tennis courts placed end-to-end.

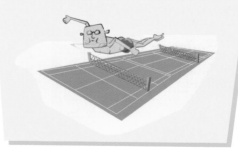

Tumble turning

ABOUT TURN

Freestyle swimmers use a technique called the 'tumble turn' to spin around at the end of each length. Just before they reach the wall of the pool, they do a half somersault. They push their heads under the water and twist their bodies around to face the other way. Then they use their legs to push off from the wall.

STROKE OF LUCK

These days, all freestyle swimmers use the front crawl, but in the past competitors have used other strokes. In 1904, Emil Rausch (GER) won the gold in the 1-mile freestyle using the sidestroke — a version of

Kieren Perkins (AUS)

MIDDLE & LONG DISTANCE FREESTYLE

The longest races are also freestyle events. These are the 400-metres, the women's 800-metres and the men's 1,500-metres.

WAY TO GO

The 400-metres freestyle is twice as long as the longest race in any other single stroke. The men's 1,500-metres is the longest race of all, though — an incredible 30 lengths of the Olympic pool! It takes great stamina, as well as great speed.

MEN'S RECORDS – WORLD: 400-metres: Paul Biedermann (GER) – 3 min. 40.07 sec. / **1,500-metres**: Sun Yang (CHN) – 14 min. 34.14 sec.
OLYMPIC: 400-metres: Ian Thorpe (AUS) – 3 min. 40.59 sec. / **1,500-metres**: Grant Hackett (AUS) – 14 min. 38.92 sec.

DID YOU KNOW?

🐋 The women's 800-metres freestyle has been won by a US swimmer on seven out of the 11 occasions that the race has been held.

🐋 Swimmers must touch the pool wall at the end of each length. In freestyle races, they may use any part of their body to do this.

🐋 In 1972 and 1976, Shirley Babashoff (USA) took part in 13 swimming races in just 8 days. She won 8 medals, including silver, in the women's 400- and 800-metres freestyle.

TWO GOLDS & TWO RECORDS

Kieren Perkins (AUS) set an Olympic record in the 1,500 metres at the 1992 Games in Barcelona. Two years later, he set a new world record in the event. Further success came in 1996, when he won another gold medal at the Games in Atlanta.

ANIMAL OLYMPIANS

When it comes to long-distance swimming, blue whales are tops. Every year, they swim up to 20,000 km, nearly twice the distance between Great Britain and Australia!

WOMEN'S RECORDS – WORLD: 400-metres: Frederica Pellegrini (ITA) – 3 min. 59.15 sec. / **800-metres**: Rebecca Adlington (GBR) – 8 min. 14.10 sec

OLYMPIC: 400-metres: Frederica Pellegrini (ITA) – 4 min. 02.19 sec. / **800-metres**: Rebecca Adlington (GBR) – 8 min. 14.10 sec.

BREASTROKE

Competitors in the 100- and 200-metres breaststroke are always looking for loopholes in the rules that will enable them to swim faster. Now the breaststroke has more regulations than any other stroke.

HANDY ADVICE

Breaststroke swimmers must touch the side of the pool with both hands at the end of every length. Failure to do so means instant disqualification!

SUPER STATS

The breaststroke is the slowest stroke. The fastest breaststroke champion has a top speed of just 6 km/h. You could run about three times as fast.

HEAD UP

About 30 years ago, breaststroke swimmers discovered they could swim faster underwater. So a new rule was introduced, which says that their heads must break the surface on every stroke — except at the start of the race or when turning.

Racing dives

WHAT A DIVE!

All swimming races (apart from backstroke events) start with the competitors diving off the starting blocks and into the pool. A good racing dive is shallow and powerful. Breaststroke swimmers often dive slightly deeper than competitors in other strokes as they are allowed to swim their first stroke underwater.

BREAST EFFORT

In the breaststroke, the swimmer's arms and legs stay underwater. Both arms move together in a circular motion, stretching out in front of the swimmer, then pushing down through the water and coming back underneath the chin. At the same time, the swimmer kicks their legs like a frog.

DID YOU KNOW?

Swimming races are started with just two commands: 'take your marks' and 'go'.

In 1936, the bronze medal in the women's 200-metres breaststroke was won by Inge Sörensen (DEN). She was only 12-years-old at the time!

If the men's 100-metres freestyle champion had a race with the 100-metres breaststroke champion, he would win by more than 10 seconds!

WOMEN'S RECORDS – WORLD: 100-metres: Jessica Hardy (USA) – 1 min. 04.45 sec / **200-metres:** Annamay Pierse (CAN) – 2 min. 20.12 sec.
OLYMPIC: 100-metres: Leisel Jones (AUS) – 1 min. 05.17 sec. / **200-metres:** Rebecca Soni (USA) – 2 min. 20.22 sec.

FLYING THE FLAG

Backstroke swimmers can't actually see where they are going! A row of flags is hung across the pool, 5 metres from each end, to warn them they are getting close to the pool wall. When turning, swimmers can use any part of their body to touch the wall.

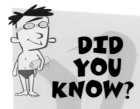

DID YOU KNOW?

An Olympic swimming lane is 2.5 metres wide.

The fastest swimmers go in the middle lanes; the slower ones get the outside lanes.

The floating lane dividers stop swimmers bumping into each other and reduce the waves created by the swimmers.

Starting a backstroke race

BACKSTROKE

The key to success in the 100- and 200-metres backstroke is to keep your body as straight as possible.

RECORD COLLECTION

Dawn Fraser isn't the only swimmer to win three Olympic golds in one event. Kristina Egerszegi (HUN) won the 200-metres backstroke event three times between 1988 and 1996, and holds five golds in all. At the 1992 Games in Barcelona, she also set two new Olympic records when she won both the 100-metres and 200-metres.

Kristina Egerszegi (HUN)

CRAWLING BACK

In the backstroke (or back crawl), swimmers must remain on their backs at all times except when turning. The leg action is the same as in the front crawl. The arms move one at a time in a circle over the swimmer's head and through the water.

WET START

Instead of diving off the starting blocks, backstroke swimmers hold on to a rail along the edge of the pool and lean back with their knees bent and their feet against the wall. When they hear the starting pistol, they launch themselves backwards by pushing off the wall with their feet.

ANIMAL OLYMPIANS

Sea otters often swim on their backs, too. In fact, they can even do it in their sleep!

BUTTERFLY

The butterfly is the newest Olympic stroke. The 100-metres event was introduced in 1956 for women and 1968 for men; the 200-metres was held for the first time in 1968 for women and 1956 for men!

ANIMAL OLYMPIANS

The massive manta ray is the butterfly champion at the Animal Olympics. It swims by beating its giant fins like underwater wings. Its fins can measure more than 6 metres across, tip-to-tip.

BALANCING ACT

Swimmers need to be very strong, especially in butterfly events. However, if their muscles become too big, they are unable to move smoothly and their swimming technique is affected. An Olympic swimmer needs to be supple, too.

MEN'S RECORDS – WORLD: 100-metres: Michael Phelps (USA) 49.82 sec. / 200-metres: Michael Phelps (USA) 1 min. 51.51 sec..
OLYMPIC: 100-metres: 100-m: Michael Phelps (USA) 50.58 sec. / 200-metres: Michael Phelps (USA) 1 min. 52.03 sec..

Denis Pankratov (RUS) won the gold in both men's butterfly events at the 1996 Games.

FLOAT LIKE A BUTTERFLY

The butterfly is the hardest stroke to master. Swimmers swing both their arms through the air then pull them down through the water. At the same time they move their legs in a 'dolphin kick', keeping their feet together while moving them up and down.

Inge De Bruijn (NED) won both freestyle titles at the 2004 Games. She won eight Olympic medals overall, including four golds. Here, she is pictured winning the women's 100m butterfly at the Sydney Olympics.

DID YOU KNOW?

)) Almost all butterfly swimmers use the dolphin kick.

)) Mary Meagher (USA) held the women's 200m butterfly world record for 19 years. Until it was broken by Susie O'Neill (AUS), Meagher's record was the longest-held record ever.

)) Kristin Otto (GDR) became the only person ever to win gold medals in three different strokes when she won the women's 100-metres butterfly, backstroke and freestyle in 1988.

WOMEN'S RECORDS – WORLD: 100-metres: Sarah Sjöström (SWE) – 56.06 sec. / **200-metres:** Liu Zige (CHN) 2 min. 01.81 sec.
OLYMPIC: 100-metres: Inge De Bruijn (NED) – 56.61 sec. / **200-metres:** Liu Zige (CHN) 2 min. 04.18 sec.

BORN SWIMMER

Michael Phelps (USA) has been a champion swimmer since the age of 15. He is currently the world record holder in the 100- and 200-metres butterfly, the 100- and 200-metres freestyle relays, the 400-metres medley and the 100-metres medley relay. He holds the Olympic record in the 200-metres freestyle and 200-metres medley.

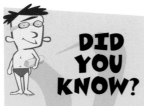

DID YOU KNOW?

❔ Tamas Darnyi (HUN) is the only person to have won both the 200-metres and 400-metres medley events at two Olympic Games.

❔ An indoor pool was first used at the Olympics in 1948. Until then, races had been held outside.

❔ Competitors can be disqualified if the judges think that their swimsuits are too skimpy!

FOUR-STROKE POWER

The medley is a four-stroke race. Competitors must use a different stroke to swim each quarter of the race, in this order: first the butterfly, next the backstroke, then the breaststroke and finally the freestyle.

CHILL OUT

According to Olympic regulations, the temperature of the water in the pool should be between 25°C and 27°C, which is slightly cooler than most public swimming pools.

MEN'S RECORDS – WORLD: **200-metres:** Ryan Lochte (USA) – 1 min. 54.00 sec. / **400-metres:** Michael Phelps (USA) – 4min. 03.84 sec.
OLYMPIC: **200-metres:** Michael Phelps (USA) – 1 min. 54.23 sec. / **400-metres:** Michael Phelps (USA) – 4 min. 03.84 sec.

MEDLEY

In the 200- and 400-metres individual medleys, each competitor must use all four different strokes.

CLOSE ENCOUNTER

The narrowest victory in Olympic history occurred in 1972, in the final of the men's 400-metres medley. Gunnar Larsson (SWE) beat Tim McKee (USA) by just two thousandths of a second — a distance of 3 mm!

SUPER STATS

BANNED!

At the 1996 Games, Michelle Smith (IRL) won gold medals in the 200-metres and 400-metres individual medleys, plus a gold in the 400-metres freestyle and a bronze in the 200-metres butterfly. However, her glory at the Olympics soon turned to disgrace when she failed a drugs test and was banned from taking part in future competitions.

Michelle Smith (IRL)

The current Olympic records in both the men's and the women's 400-metres individual medleys are now more than 40 seconds faster than the winning times when the races were first held in 1964 — that's long enough to do another length!

OMEN'S RECORDS – WORLD: 200-metres: Ariana Kukors (USA) – 2 min. 06.15 sec. / **400-metres**: Stephanie Rice (AUS) – 4 min. 29.45 sec.
OLYMPIC: 200-metres: Stephanie Rice (AUS) – 4 min. 08.45 sec.. / **400-metres**: Stephanie Rice (AUS) – 4 min. 29.45 sec..

RELAY

Teams of four swimmers each swim a quarter of the race in the 4 x 100-metres freestyle, 4 x 200-metres freestyle and 4 x 100-metres medley relays.

CLEAN SWEEP

Historically, the USA has always dominated the relays. At the 1996 Atlanta Olympics, US swimmers won every one of the six races. The women's 4 x 100-metre freestyle team set new Olympic records in 1996 and 2000, only to be beaten by the Australian team in 2004.

SUPER STATS

There have been a total of 85 relay races held at Olympics. The USA has won 60 of them.

MEDLEY MIX

In the medley relay, each member of the team uses a different stroke. The first swimmer swims with the backstroke, the second with the breaststroke, the third with the butterfly and the fourth swims freestyle.

MEN'S RECORDS - WORLD: 4 x 100-metres fr.: USA – 3 min. 08.24 sec. / 4 x 200-metres fr.: USA – 6 min. 58.56 sec. / 4 x 100-metres m.r.: USA – 3 min 27.28 sec.

OLYMPIC: 4 x 100-metres fr.: USA – 3 min. 08.24 sec. / 4 x 200-metres fr.: USA – 6 min. 58.56 sec. / 4 x 100-metres m.r.: USA – 3 min. 29.34 sec.

GO APE, MAN

The 4 x 200-metres freestyle relays in 1924 and 1928 were won by the team from the USA. One of the members of that team was Johnny Weissmuller, the greatest swimmer of his day. He won a total of five Olympic golds and eventually went on to become a famous film star — by playing Tarzan in the Hollywood movies!

Johnny Weissmuller as Tarzan

1996 US women's 4 x 100-metres freestyle team

DID YOU KNOW?

🎽 The US men's teams have won the 4 X 100-metres freestyle the 7 out of 9 times it has been held.

🎽 Eleanor Holm (USA), who won the 100-metres backstroke in 1932, starred as Tarzan's girlfriend, Jane, in a film made in 1938.

🎽 The oldest person to win a medal in any swimming event was 46-year-old William Henry (GBR), who won a bronze in the 1906 freestyle relay.

WAIT FOR IT!

During relay races, each swimmer must wait for their team-mate to touch the wall before diving in. If a swimmer starts too soon, the whole team is disqualified.

DIVING

iving has been part of the Olympics since 1904. At the 2000 Games two new synchronized diving events were introduced.

TAKE FIVE

There are five basic types of dive, known as forward, backward, reverse, inward and twist. However, there are more than 100 recognized variations. Divers try to impress the judges by performing gymnastic moves, such as somersaults, tucks and pikes, in mid-air.

Jenny Keim & Kathy Pesek (USA)

IT'S A SYNCH

Synchronized diving is when two divers perform together. The idea is that both divers mirror one another as closely as possible and they are then judged as a pair. There are springboard and platform synchronized competitions.

Greg Louganis (USA)

OUCH!

While attempting a reverse dive at the 1988 Olympics, Greg Louganis (USA) hit his head on the springboard and was badly injured. However, he refused to pull out of the competition and, with his head still in bandages, went on to win his fourth Olympic gold medal!

SPRING INTO ACTION

Olympic diving competitions include both springboard and platform events. The springboard is just 3 metres above the pool and is very flexible. By jumping on it, competitors can spring high into the air. You can find out about platform diving on pages 22–23.

ANIMAL OLYMPIANS

At the Animal Olympics, the sperm whale would win the diving by a mile – or a mile-and-a-half (2.4 km) to be precise. That's how deep these huge creatures can dive in search of something to eat.

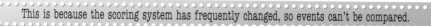

This is because the scoring system has frequently changed, so events can't be compared.

DIVING
(CONTINUED)

Dmitri Sautin (RUS)

The platform dive takes strength, courage and balance.

NEED A HAND?

Here, 1996 Olympic platform champion, Dmitri Sautin (RUS), is shown performing an armstand dive, which is only made from the platform. Competitors start by doing a handstand at the very edge of the board, then push off with their arms.

GOLDEN AGE

On the 1996 Games, then 17 years old Mingxia Fu (CHN) was the fourth female to capture both the platform and springboard events. In 1991, she became the youngest-ever world diving champion — at the age of 11! Since then, the rules have changed; now all divers in both world and Olympic competitions must be at least 14-years-old.

ANIMAL OLYMPIANS

As platform divers hit the water, they are falling through the air at up to 55 km/h. When peregrine falcons dive down on their unsuspecting prey, they reach speeds of around 350 km/h.

There is no such thing as a world or Olympic record for diving.

10 metres platform board

7.5 metres platform boards (not used in Olympic competitions)

5 metres platform boards (not used in Olympic competitions)

3 metres springboards

A jet of water causes tiny ripples on the surface of the pool underneath the diving boards. Without it, the divers would not be able to see where the water began.

DID YOU KNOW?

🏅 Klaus Dibiasi (ITA) won the platform competition in 1968, 1972 and 1976 – the only Olympic diver to have won the same event 3 times in a row.

🏅 The platform dive is also known as the highboard – for obvious reasons!

🏅 The first Olympic diving competition for women was held in 1912.

JUDGE & JURY

The individual diving events are judged by a panel of seven judges. Nine judges score the synchronized dives. The number of points per dive is awarded as follows: first, the judges mark each dive out of 10 for performance; then they multiply their scores by a number according to the difficulty of the dive – the harder the dive the higher the number.

This is because the scoring system has frequently changed, so events can't be compared.

GAME ON

Each water polo match consists of four bouts of eight minutes and there are two referees to ensure fair play. The pool must be 30 metres long, 20 metres wide and at least 1.8 metres deep. The court is marked out with lines painted on the bottom of the pool.

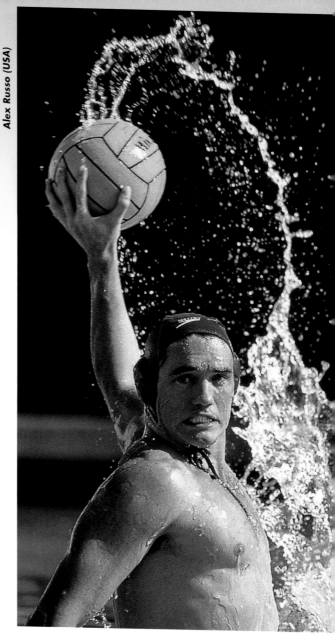

Alex Russo (USA)

DID YOU KNOW?

The first-ever Olympic water polo tournament was won by the Osborne Swimming Club from Manchester, representing Great Britain.

A member of the winning Hungarian team in 1932 and 1936 had only one leg.

In 1968, the team from the German Democratic Republic beat their opponents from the United Arab Emirates by 19–2: a record score!

TOUGH PLAY

To play water polo, competitors need the stamina of a long-distance swimmer, the accuracy of a football player and the strength of a wrestler.

WATER POLO

ater polo was first played at the Olympics in 1900. It was the only team sport at the early Games apart from football.

POLO CRAZY

Water polo is a bit like an aquatic version of football. Each side has seven players and the idea is to score as many points as possible by throwing the ball into the opposition's goal. Players may only use one hand when passing or shooting, and no one except the goalkeeper is allowed to touch the bottom or sides of the pool.

Men's water polo

SUPER STATS

Hungary has won the Olympic water polo tournament more times than any other country, with nine victories to its credit. Great Britain and Italy are second with four wins, while the former Yugoslavia is in third place with three wins.

HUNGARY	|||||||||
GREAT BRITAIN	||||
ITALY	||||
YUGOSLAVIA	|||

MAD HATTERS

Players wear coloured hats to show which side they are on. Usually one team wears white and the other blue. Goalkeepers usually wear red hats. The hats have chin straps to stop them being pulled off, and ear protectors.

This is because the objective is to win rather than to achieve as high a score as possible.

WATER POLO
(CONTINUED)

Water polo was a male-only sport at the Games until the 2000 Sydney Games, when women were allowed to compete for the first time.

ONES TO WATCH

The women's team from the Netherlands won in the 2008 Olympics when it beat the USA 9–8. The very first Olympic final for women was also close, with the USA again losing, on this occasion 4–3 to Australia.

SUPER STATS

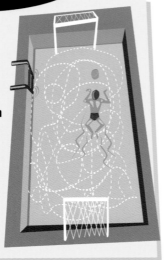

Water polo players can often swim up to 5 km during a match.

BLOCK TACTICS

When defending, players try to block the other team's shots using their arms and body. By kicking furiously with their legs (remember, they are not allowed to touch the bottom of the pool), they try to leap out of the water in front of the attacker just as they throw the ball. It takes great strength — and great timing!

There is no such thing as a world or Olympic record for water polo.

GET OUT OF THE POOL

Water polo is a rough, physical sport, but players are not allowed to dunk or hold on to each other. Fouls can result in players being sent out of the pool for 20 seconds; three such offences usually means they stay out for the rest of the match!

FREE THROWS

As in football, if the ball goes out of play (in this case, if it lands outside the pool) the team that touched it last is penalized and the other team is given a throw-in. Free throws are also awarded in the event of a foul. If a serious offence is committed by one side, its opponents are given a free shot just 5 metres away from the goal.

Maureen O' Toole (USA) & Gillian Vanden Berg (NED)

DID YOU KNOW?

Water polo players are not allowed to wear goggles.

In addition to the two referees, there are several other officials whose job it is to watch out for fouls.

Each team is allowed to make four substitutions during a match.

This is because the objective is to win rather than to achieve as high a score as possible.

28

WATER MUSIC

Speakers in the wall of the pool enable the competitors to hear the music while they are underwater. This makes it possible for swimmers to move together with split-second timing.

DID YOU KNOW?

♫ The synchro duet was held in 1984–1992, but not at the 1996 Olympics.

♫ In 1992, the winners of both the gold and the silver medals were twins: Karen and Sarah Josephson (USA) won the gold, and Penny and Vicky Vilagos (CAN) the silver.

♫ Japan has won medals in the duet event in every Olympic final!

Olga Brousnikina (RUS)

GOLD OLGA

Canada and the United States have been the traditional winners in the synchronized events. However, in the last two Olympic Games Russia has come out on top, winning both the duet and team events. Olga Brousnikina, pictured, shows how it's done.

SYNCHRO DUET

Synchronized swimming appeared as an exhibition event at the Olympics in 1952–1968, before becoming a full medal sport in 1984.

BEAUTY TIPS

Competitors use waterproof lipstick and make-up to help them look their best. Instead of wearing a swimming cap, some swimmers put gelatin on their hair. This means their hair stays perfectly in place, even underwater!

SHALL WE DANCE?

Synchro began in Canada in the 1920s and was originally called water ballet. Like ballet, it involves moving to music, but instead of dancing, competitors perform in water. Only women are allowed to compete in synchro, which makes it the only swimming discipline with no men's event.

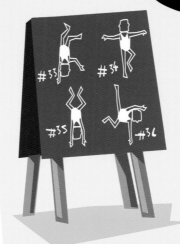

SUPER STATS

There are almost 200 different recognized moves in synchronized swimming. So if you practised four a week, it would take you almost a whole year to learn them all.

SYNCHRO TEAM

The team competition was introduced for the first time at the 1996 Olympics. Each team is made up of eight swimmers.

PART ONE...

Both the duet and the team events are made up of two parts. The first is a technical routine, in which competitors must perform specific moves in a certain order and within a set time.

...AND PART TWO!

The second part of the competition is a free routine without restrictions. This gives the swimmers a chance to show off their skills with as much imagination as possible.

Synchronized swimming team (NED)

ANIMAL OLYMPIANS

Herrings are the synchro swimming champions of the animal kingdom. They swim together in huge groups (called 'schools') sometimes comprising several million fish, with each one following almost exactly the movements of the rest.

WINNING BY A NOSE (CLIP)

A nose clip is the most essential piece of equipment that synchro swimmers need. It prevents water from entering their nose, helping them to hold their breath and stay submerged for longer. Competitors are also allowed to wear a swimming cap and goggles if they wish.

Synchronized swimmer

MAKING YOUR POINT

Two panels of five judges award points for each part of the competition. One panel scores the execution of the moves — how well they are performed. The other panel scores the overall performance — how beautifully the different moves are linked together.

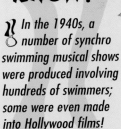

DID YOU KNOW?

❓ In the 1940s, a number of synchro swimming musical shows were produced involving hundreds of swimmers; some were even made into Hollywood films!

❓ Boosts, rockets, thrusts and twirls are all names for different synchro moves.

❓ Until 1992, there was also a solo synchro competition for individual medallists.

INDEX

Acknowledgements

Copyright © Wise Walrus 2000, 2008, 2012
This revised edition published in 2012 by Wise Walrus.
First published in Great Britain in 2000 by TickTock Entertainment Ltd.
The Pantiles Chambers, 85 High Street, Tunbridge Wells, Kent TN1 1XP, UK.
ISBN: 978-1-84898-541-4
Printed in China   10 9 8 7 6 5 4 3 2 1
Sports Consultant: Andrew Raeburn.   Cartoons by John Alston.
We would like to thank Ian Hodge, Rosalind Beckman, Jackie Gaff, Ben Hubbard and Elizabeth Wiggans for their assistance.

A CIP catalogue record for this book is available from the British Library.
All rights reserved. No part of this publication may be reproduced, stored in a retrieval system, or transmitted in any form or by any means electronic, mechanical, photocopying, recording or otherwise, without prior written permission of the copyright owner.

Picture Credits: t =top, b =bottom, c =centre, l =left, r =right, OFC =outside front cover, OBC =outside back cover, IFC =inside front cover

Allsport: IFC, 2/3t, 3b, 4/5t, 5b, 6/7 (main pic), 7tr, 8tr, 8/9c, 10/11t, 12/13 (main pic), 13tr, 15t, 16/17b, 18/19c, 20tl, 20/21 (main pic), 22l, 22/23t, 24/25 (main pic), 25t, 26/27b, 28/29t, 28/29b, 30/31c, 31tr. Daniel Berehulak/ Getty Images for FINA: 14/15b. Giuliano Bevilacqua/ Rex Features: 16/17t. Adam Davy/ EMPICS Sport/ PA Photos: 10/11b. Getty Images: OFC. Ronald Grant Archive; 19tr. Reuters/ Andy Clark SN/AA: 26/27t. Cover: Corbis (main image), Shutterstock (top and bottom right)

Picture research by Image Select.